REVOLUTION, NOT REFORM

by Jordan Levi

ISBN 978-1-7340861-3-3

Dedicated to Earth and all of its offspring past, present, and future. May we make it through these trying times with sound reason.

"In modern agriculture, as in the urban industries, the increased productiveness and quantity of the labour set in motion are bought at the cost of laying waste and consuming by disease labour-power itself. Moreover, all progress in capitalistic agriculture is a progress in the art, not only of robbing the labourer, but of robbing the soil; all progress in increasing the fertility of the soil for a given time, is a progress towards ruining the lasting sources of that fertility. The more a country starts its development on the foundation of modern industry, like the United States, for example, the more rapid is this process of destruction. Capitalist production, therefore, develops technology, and the combining together of various processes into a social whole, only by sapping the original sources of all wealth-the soil and the labourer"

-Karl Marx, Capital, Volume 1, Chapter 15, Section 10

Table of Contents

Acknowledgments

I'd like to first thank Karl Marx and Friedrich Engels for their invaluable contribution to socialist theory. Thanks as well to every past, present, and future member of the World Socialist Movement for keeping the original concept of socialism alive. In particular, thanks to Michael Schauerte for doing the bulk of the editing, to Stephen Shenfield for his help editing and for writing the Foreword, to Robin Cox for his feedback, as well as to the late Karla Rab for giving a talk that I have quoted. I'd also like to thank everyone who contributed to the sources I reference. Finally, thank you to my twin brother, Roméo Levi, for helping me get over a bout of discouragement as I wrote this and to my soulmate, Susana Orozco-Martinez, for her feedback as well. This pamphlet wouldn't have been possible without all of you.

Foreword

The title of this pamphlet, taken in isolation, may cause misunderstanding.

We socialists are not opposed to reforms as such. Any reform should be judged on its merits. Some reforms are in the interest of humanity and the working class. Anyone who has lived, as I have, both in the United States and in a country with a national health service will appreciate the potential benefits of a scheme like Bernie's Medicare For All.

Aiming to achieve socialism by democratic means, we socialists support reforms that defend, strengthen, or extend democracy by, for instance, abolishing the Electoral College, blocking the removal of black voters from electoral rolls, or guaranteeing media access for small parties. The political system of the United States is a mix of democratic and plutocratic elements – a far cry from full democracy.

What we socialists oppose is not reforms as such but reform-*ism* – a political approach that concentrates on campaigning for reforms within the existing system. Reformists ignore or at best sideline the need for systemic change. When they get elected to public office on the basis of a program of reforms, they are forced by circumstances to manage capitalism and submit to its imperatives, often at the expense of reforms that they promised to implement.

The trouble is that most beneficial reforms go against the grain of the capitalist drive for profit. Even if they are implemented, capitalists will therefore seek and usually find ways to water down, evade, subvert, and sabotage them. Eventually they may be reversed altogether. Indeed, many reforms won in the US at earlier periods are now being reversed. Reformists have to fight the same battles over and over again. They toil endlessly on 'the treadmill of reform' but make little or no *sustained* progress.

We socialists consider it more sensible and promising to strike directly at the root of most of the problems facing humanity and the working class – capitalism. We set our sights on 'Revolution, Not Reform.'

Stephen D. Shenfield
General Secretary, World Socialist Party of the US

Preface

I'd like to start off by saying thank you for taking the time to read this pamphlet. Whether you're reading it to get a better understanding of what socialism truly is or to debunk my arguments, I genuinely appreciate it, because the only way we're able to make progress in society is through objective discussion.

I wrote this pamphlet because I feel like there's a general confusion among average citizens about what socialism actually is. I've heard the mainstream media refer to anyone from the Nazis to Bernie Sanders as "socialists," and the stark difference between the two obviously left me with some burning questions. I was a huge supporter of Bernie during his 2016 presidential campaign because I felt at the time he was addressing core issues. My impression was that he was not another rich man's puppet and was genuinely trying to improve conditions for the working class.

However, hearing so many people say that his policies would turn America into the next Venezuela and not having an adequate rebuttal to that argument made me realize I was too focused on his policy solutions and not the actual idea of socialism. This naturally led me to read up on socialism from the source and try to figure out what may have gone wrong with the alleged attempts at establishing it before.

Reading some works by Karl Marx quickly made me realize the enormous difference between his idea of socialism and what Bernie was talking about doing or what other countries had done.

Searching the internet to find other people or groups who recognized this clear difference eventually led me to the Socialist Party of Great Britain's website(spgb.net). Reading through many of their articles helped me understand and better articulate the true meaning of socialism. However, knowing many people might not want to wade through all the stuff I read on the SPGB website, I wanted to summarize as much as possible in one place. While there will still be people who won't care to listen, I figured helping *anybody* understand this would be well worth the effort.

First and foremost, you'd be doing yourself a great disservice by accepting any of this information as true without doing further research. I implore every single person who reads to validate all my sources themselves. To do otherwise would be arming yourself with empty knowledge.

Secondly, I welcome anyone to try to debunk me on this. If I'm wrong, I'd like to know that more than anything. My only allegiance is to facts and sound reason, and if I'm proven wrong, I'd like to correct my position as soon as possible. However, I feel the need to stress that discrediting anything other than the information provided is not a valid rebuttal. Ad hominem arguments, for example, won't cut it, family.

If you have any questions or concerns or would just like to give general feedback, I've included the contact info for the World Socialist Movement's various branches. My contact info is also on my webpage at https://bluelotusent.com/swaminetero.

So, without further ado, let's begin our discussion.

Introduction: Dystopia

Stagnant real wages;[1] Rising cost of living;[2] Technological unemployment;[3] Anthropogenic climate change.[4]

You could almost be forgiven for mistaking modern society for an animated George Orwell novel. Things right now are looking *bleak*. If I didn't know any better, I'd swear we're all on a worldwide episode of *Punk'd*. You mean to tell me that 78% of US workers live paycheck-to-paycheck,[5] and 80% of Americans are in debt,[6] and we *still* don't have flying cars? This isn't the future I was promised, and I'd like to speak to the manager expeditiously.

It seems like there's a new apocalyptic conspiracy every year, but this climate change one just hits a little different, my guy. It's not some decrepit rock backing this one up, there's actual science behind it, and people are freaking out accordingly. They're starting to recognize the fact that it's not a game this time and if we keep electing politicians who make empty campaign promises to win, humanity might not survive to see 2100. Almost a fourth of US workers already don't receive any paid vacations or holidays,[7] but to find out that all of that hard work might be in vain if we don't live to see retirement?

We're *worried*. In a world that seems to be on the brink of collapse, it'd be strange for someone *not* to be concerned. So, when politicians come along proposing policies that appear to address problems like rising levels of wealth inequality[8] and collapsing ecosystems,[9] it's understandable that many working-class citizens rally in support. Whether those measures make economic sense or not, at least they sound like an effort to genuinely help the *people* for once, not just the corporations. That's a breath of fresh air, considering the last president to do that was *easily* FDR, who died in office in 1945 – the same year world War II ended. Bernie Sanders and Alexandria Ocasio-Cortez are the only glimpses of hope many Americans have ever had.

I appreciate that they've helped "socialism" to not be considered such a dirty word anymore. I also completely understand the average person's confusion about exactly what socialism is, given the misinformation about it generated by the major media outlets. However, Bernie, AOC, and Jeremy Corbyn are unfortunately contributing more to the confusion – even if only accidentally – by calling themselves "democratic socialists," which is a redundant term to anyone with even a basic understanding of genuine socialism. That's like someone calling themselves an authoritarian fascist or an anti-statist libertarian.

Socialism is, *by definition*, democratic. A socialist political candidate would be subject to the democratic will of members of a socialist party, and all of them would understand that time spent on trying to reform capitalism would be time *not* spent on establishing socialism, since the two are mutually exclusive. To campaign for reforms contradicts their primary goal. A "socialist" who doesn't understand this isn't a socialist at all, and that's the key difference between socialism and reformism. Socialists fight for socialism now, while reformists fight to reform capitalism and believe socialism will arrive once enough reforms have been implemented. That is impossible, however, because socialism is a completely different economic system, completely incompatible with capitalism. Socialism can never be achieved by trying to make capitalism more humane. Not only has that failed multiple times, but it's contrary to the nature of capitalism itself. Vast inequality is a requirement for capitalism to work properly. But to truly understand this, we first need a basic understanding of what capitalism is.

What Is Capitalism?

Capitalism is an economic system based on private owner-ship of the means of production and production for profit.[10] Capitalism requires a poor majority of individuals who are forced to live off of the wages they earn by selling their labor power to operate the means of production to produce com-modities. This is the *working class*. Meanwhile, there is a rich minority of individuals who live off the profits generated by the labor exerted by the workers in the production process. This is the *capitalist class*.[11] Sounds eerily similar to slavery or serfdom, doesn't it?

Anyway, in that sense, capitalism requires the develop-ment of: private property(meaning capital, which is used to generate profit, being different from personal property, which isn't used for that purpose),[12] money(as a means of purchase),[13] wages(which are used to buy labor power and sustain the working class),[14] commodities(which you buy with the money),[15] classes(whose interests are diametrically opposed),[16] a state(to protect the interests of the capital-ist class),[17] and leaders(to make decisions for the working class).[18]

For capitalism to work properly, there always needs to be a vast majority of people whose best means of survival is to earn wages through employment, and a small minority of people who finesse their employees by paying them less than the value they create to extract profit they then use to cover their living expenses and reinvest part of as well in the hopes that they'll accumulate more capital. Think exploitation, but legal. If there were more capitalists than workers, there wouldn't be a large enough supply of labor power to meet the demand for it. The interests of both classes are also completely opposed, because it's in the workers' best interest to earn the highest wages possible, while it's in the capitalist's best interest to pay the lowest wages possible.[19] If wages are too high, capitalists can't make enough profit to sustain the system, and if wages are too low, workers won't earn enough for them or their families to survive.

Profits are priority #1 within a capitalist economy, because without them the system can't run properly. Profit is literally the oil to capitalism's engine. Capitalists #1 concern is keeping profits as high as possible, so they can stay competitive within the market. That requires capitalists to cut costs as much as possible, which can mean anything ranging from committing various forms of wage theft – which may cost workers up to 3x as much as the largest Ponzi scheme in world history every year –[20][21] to not purchasing optional safety mechanisms on an airplane since they'll cost more money, causing at least 2 airplanes to crash and kill more than 150 passengers each.[22] That includes allowing almost 15,000 children under 5 years old to die of starvation every day,[23] while the world wastes enough food in *one day* to feed *all* of them for a *year*.[24] That includes allowing around 2.5 million children to be homeless in America every year,[25] the same country that has more than double that number of abandoned homes: around 5.6 million.[26] That includes 60 of America's Fortune 500 companies paying no federal income tax in 2018,[27] while most of them pay their employees less than a living wage, forcing many of them to receive welfare,[28] essentially causing taxpayers to pick up the slack. I could do this *all day*, chief.

Profit takes precedence over environmental safety, human lives, ethics – *everything*, because it has to in a capitalist economy, or the entire system will implode. Nothing can ever take priority over profit within a capitalist economy and nothing can ever change that within one. Anyone who tells you different is a liar. For humanity, the environment, or anything to ever be priority #1, we'd have to establish a completely different type of economic system where profit doesn't exist in the first place.

What Is Socialism?

Socialism is an economic system based on common ownership of the means of production and production for use. [29] It's worth noting that, while Karl Marx sometimes used the term "communism" and Friedrich Engels used the term "scientific socialism" to differentiate their ideology from utopian socialism, they frequently used the terms communism and socialism interchangeably throughout their work. They by no means thought these were different concepts or different stages in development.[30] In "Critique of the Gotha Programme," Karl Marx differentiated between a "first" and "higher" stage of communism,[31] but in "The State and Revolution," Vladimir Lenin turned this into a differentiation between socialism and communism instead.[32] Leninism is the source of this, as well as many other misconceptions of socialism, but we'll delve more into that later. SPOILER ALERT: he distorted *all* of it.

Socialism requires everything in society to either be personal or common property so that all our resources would be freely accessible and calculated in kind, with all citizens having equal say in how they're distributed and utilized. Think of how everything's used at your home but imagine that, uh ... *worldwide*. In this form of an economy, there would be no: private property(since everything would be owned either personally or in common),[33] money(since nothing would be for sale),[34] wages(since there'd be no money),[35] commodities(since everything would be produced directly for use, rather than for sale),[36] classes(since everything would be owned equally),[37] state(at least not in the current sense, since the government wouldn't have any class interests to protect),[38] or leaders(since an economy based on equal ownership and free access would also be a direct democracy)[39]. The World Socialist Movement defines this positively as "a democracy in which free and equal men and women co-operate to produce the things they need to live and enjoy life, to which they have free access in accordance with the principle 'from each according to their abilities, to each according to their needs'".

The defining characteristic of a socialist economy is production for use. While commodities are produced with the intent to be used in a capitalist economy, they aren't produced directly for use, they're produced directly with the intent to realize a profit. While commodities are sometimes sold at a loss, that's only an exception to the rule. Regardless of how badly a commodity is needed, it will only be produced and exchanged if there are people willing and able to pay for it at a price that will realize an acceptable profit for the producer. Economics calls this "effective demand,"[40] but I prefer to call it "solicitation of prostitution." This artificial barrier of profit is the sole cause of innumerable deaths from malnutrition, starvation, treatable diseases, and more, all because there was not "effective demand" among the victims for necessities like food, clean water, or proper medication.

In a socialist economy, based on production for use, this artificial barrier of profit would be eliminated. There would no longer be such things as money, wages, or commodities, because nothing would be for sale in the first place. There would be universal free access to all the necessities of life, so that death by starvation or treatable diseases would be impossible. That means every plane would have the necessary safety mechanisms, eliminating the sorts of crashes caused by penny pinching. That means no more involuntary starvation. That means no more involuntary homelessness. That means no one being forced to live off of less than they need. Again, I could do this *all day*, chief.

As you can see, this is the exact opposite of capitalism, which is why the two systems are completely incompatible. Anyone claiming to desire a "socialism" that has any of the defining characteristics of capitalism doesn't want socialism at all; they just want a different form of capitalism. They want capitalism with reforms, which isn't the same thing as socialism at all. Socialism is a completely different, post-capitalist system that can't be established by retaining any of the main characteristics of capitalism. Anyone that says otherwise is either misinformed or an outright liar, bruh.

Socialism vs. Reformism

Now that we've established the differences between socialism and capitalism, let's look at some of Bernie Sanders's policies for his 2020 presidential campaign and see if any of these can be considered socialist, shall we? It'd take too long to break down every issue, so I'll just briefly address a few.

Bernie made demands: for the wealthy, large corporations and Wall Street to pay their fair share in taxes,[41] for "real Wall Street reform"[42] and "fair banking for all"[43]. In other words, he still wants there to be private property and money, but just wants corporations and banks to be more ethical. He talked about "fighting for working families"[44], which shows that he assumes there will still be wages and classes, but just wants workers to be paid more. Instead of universal free access in general, his slogans are "health care for all"[45] and "college for all"[46]. So it's safe to say he still wants there to be commodities, but just wants universal free healthcare and tuition-free public colleges and universities. And when he says "get big money out of politics and restore democracy"[47] we can assume that he still wants a state and leaders, but just wants them to be more ethical. Not once does he demand anything even remotely similar to the Object of the World Socialist Movement: "The establishment of a system of society based upon the common ownership and democratic control of the means and instruments for producing and distributing wealth by and in the interest of the whole community."[48]

To call any of these policies "socialist" isn't only wrong, it's flat out delusional. Some of the Nordic countries have implemented similar measures, and they're correct to still classify themselves as capitalist.[49] All of these measures require the preservation of capitalism, which is the exact opposite of socialism. Fighting for a fairer form of capitalism isn't the same thing as fighting for socialism. Let me be very clear: I believe Bernie's heart is in the right place, but he doesn't want to establish socialism; he wants capitalism to be reformed.

Reformists sometimes argue that fighting for enough reforms will eventually lead to socialism, but all of them eventually abandon the goal of socialism altogether and only focus on reforms. This is because reformism requires the preservation of capitalism, whereas socialism requires its destruction. You obviously can't fight for two contradictory goals simultaneously. Reformism is a slippery slope that has inevitably led to the abandonment of socialism, time and time again. One of the most notable examples of this is the Social Democratic Party of Germany, which Karl Marx criticized in his aforementioned work, 'Critique of the Gotha Program' for this very reason. They adopted this reformist program, claiming to want to abolish capitalism,[50] but that party later abandoned that goal entirely with the ratification of the "Godesberg Program" in 1959, which rejected their initial goal of replacing capitalism and committed to merely reforming it.[51]

Another reformist measure that seems to be generating some confusion is the concept of a Universal Basic Income, or UBI. I've never heard anyone refer to it as "socialist," but I have heard it described as "post-capitalist". While UBI will be of some benefit at least to unemployed workers, it won't even come close to solving the problems of capitalism, because it will leave the profit motive intact and exert a downward pressure on wages, lowering them by as much as is given to each individual on average. In other words, it's basically a subsidy for the capitalist class. This can be proven from experience, since it's exactly what happened when a similar measure – the Speenhamland system – was implemented in Speenhamland, England in 1795.[52] Due to distress caused by high grain prices, the Speenhamland authorities approved a wage supplement to offset the crisis. The system failed because it allowed employers to pay lower wages since the parish would make up the difference, leaving the workers' income effectively the same and the poor rate contributors essentially subsidizing the employer's wage payments. Sorry, Yang Gang.

It's also worth noting that Bernie Sanders endorsed the passing of a "Green New Deal," something Alexandria Ocasio-Cortez recently sponsored resolutions for to the House and Senate. While I don't recall seeing anyone calling that policy "socialist" either, the fact that she calls herself a "democratic socialist" may still cause some confusion. In her resolutions,[53] the policy's primary goals include: "...providing and leveraging...adequate capital (including through...public banks, and other public financing)...and other forms of assistance to...Federal, State, and local government agencies..." – meaning they still want money, a state, and leaders, they just want more money for them; "...guaranteeing a job with a family-sustaining wage..." – meaning they still want classes and wages, they just want wages to be higher; "ensuring a commercial environment where every businessperson is free from unfair competition and domination by domestic or international monopolies" – meaning they still want private property, they just want small and big businesses to have a level playing field; and "...providing all people of the United States with...affordable...housing...and affordable food..." – meaning they still want commodities, they just want them to be cheaper. Sounds pretty capitalist to me.

Aside from that, we should take special note of the fact that the primary goal of the program is to curb climate change. The issue of climate change itself is too extensive to go into in depth here, but the gist is that a vast majority of scientists agree – based on mountains of scientific evidence[54] – that human beings are the main cause of a rapid rise in carbon and greenhouse gas emissions over the past 200 years[55] and that we need to drastically reduce emissions by 2030 at the latest and reach zero emissions by 2050,[56] to mitigate what could be grave, more than likely irreversible environmental consequences.[57] Exactly how severe the consequences might be is heavily debated, but most scientists agree that they won't be negligible. Many of the scientists who disagree are trained not in climate science but in a different scientific field and are therefore not real experts, and I suspect any climate scientists who disagree are either paid to or missing some brain cells.

The necessary changes to our entire infrastructure could cost trillions of dollars.[58] That's money that the capitalist class doesn't want to pay. It's in their best interest to keep profits as high as possible, even if it means endangering the environment and human lives in the process. Any legislation to cut back on emissions will be worked around, and it already has,[59] because capitalists would rather have a yacht than a planet to ride it on. Even if the capitalist class were to fully comply, they'd likely opt to utilize more "cost effective" methods like reforestation – which could take decades and may only make a significant difference if done on a sufficiently large scale[60] – and stratospheric aerosol injection – which would only postpone climate change and could even cause worse problems.[61] While other methods like direct air capture of greenhouse gases for their creation into biofuel would be more effective,[62] they're also potentially much more expensive,[63] and as long as cost is a barrier, the safety of the planet and the human race will always come second. If we want to solve this problem as fast and as effectively as possible, our only option is to eliminate the factor of cost entirely.

Socialism vs. State Capitalism

It'd be foolish of me not to address the elephant in the room, the alleged "socialist" and "communist" revolutions of the 20th century. To reiterate: capitalism is based on private ownership of the means of production and production for profit, whereas socialism is based on common ownership of the means of production and production for use. Private ownership is the polar opposite of common ownership and production for profit is the polar opposite of production for use. A capitalist economy requires private property, money, commodities, classes, wages, a state, and leaders and a socialist economy wouldn't have any of these.

Before Vladimir Lenin led the Bolshevik Revolution in 1917, this was largely understood. However, after the Bolsheviks claimed their movement was "communist" the public understanding of that term changed. It was in Russia's best interest to take control of and capitalize on a rising interest in communism, and it was in America's best interest to demonize communism, since it was a threat to the establishment and there was a rising interest in it here, too. With all the major media outlets of the time classifying the revolution as "communist," no one would question it if they didn't already know any better. But that common perception, was wrong. As the World Socialist Movement even pointed out at that time, this revolution couldn't properly be defined as communist at all, because Russian citizens weren't prepared for communism yet.[64] That's why Lenin's ideology isn't considered part of orthodox Marxism, but rather a completely separate strain called Marxism-Leninism, because it changed key tenets of Marxism. Russia still had money, wages, commodities, classes, a state, and leaders. The only difference was that the means of production – all the commercial property – was no longer privately owned by individual citizens, but rather the property of the state itself. Individual citizens no longer accumulated profit, but the state did. The capitalist class was no longer made up of individual citizens, but of state bureaucrats. This was still capitalism in nature, but a reformed version – *state capitalism*. Lenin even admitted that Russia's economy wasn't socialist in an article.[65]

This fact holds true without fail for every self-proclaimed "socialist" or "communist" nation that has ever existed or continues to exist today. Russia's economy was fully nationalized from 1928[66] to 1988,[67] China's was fully nationalized from 1956[68] to 1979,[69] Cuba's was fully nationalized from 1963[70] to 1992,[71] North Korea's was fully nationalized from 1958[72] to 1998,[73] etc. They all have or had a majority, more or less, of state ownership of the means of production, wherein the state undertook production for profit. Just because they call themselves socialist or communist doesn't mean that's what they are. If that were the case, then everybody would have to consider The Democratic People's Republic of Korea(North Korea) a democracy instead of a dictatorship. If a country has all the characteristics of a state capitalist economy, then that's what their economy is, regardless of what they want to call it.

One of the more recent countries that have perpetrated this misconception is Venezuela, leading to the notoriously nauseating "Argumentum ad Venezuelam" many people mistakenly use to discredit the idea of a socialist economy. While I wouldn't really call its economy state capitalist since the private sector's contribution to the country's GDP is 71%[74] – something that people using that argument are frequently unaware of. I'd agree with it being more similar to what I've seen called "left-wing capitalism," in contrast with countries like the US, for example, where the private sector's contribution to the country's GDP is 89%.[75] It's not majority state-owned like other countries I've mentioned, but it definitely has more state ownership than the average capitalist economy.

Once those facts are understood, it becomes clear how absurd it is to argue that Venezuela's economic disaster was caused by socialism. That can't possibly be true if their economy was never socialist – or even fully nationalized – in the first place. The natural process of thought would be to then ask: well then what was it caused by? A big part of the answer is economic sanctions imposed by the US, but unpacking this topic would require a whole other pamphlet.

Aside from all of this, the most important thing to understand is that socialism can't exist in one country alone. From the very beginning, Karl Marx and Friedrich Engels made it very clear that a socialist country couldn't supply all their resources themselves or resist pressure if every other country is capitalist, so socialism could only exist worldwide – meaning its implementation by all the most developed countries in the world, at a very minimum.[76] Now, the next question is if that's possible.

Is Socialism Practical?

After someone understands that socialism and capitalism are polar opposites that can't coexist, and that any country that has ever claimed to be socialist or communist was actually capitalist, they're likely to call the idea of a genuine socialist society impractical, for various reasons. Here I'd like to just touch on what I consider to be the main criticisms of socialist theory.

Possibly the most common argument is that socialism's somehow against human nature. There are a couple things to unpack here, but we'll start with the implication that capitalism is in accordance with human nature. Something many people who believe this tend to be unaware of is that the working class didn't just walk into modern capitalism voluntarily; they were forced into it kicking and screaming. Karl Marx addressed the first volume of *Capital*, where he mentioned the Highland Clearances.[77] This was a process in which big landowners evicted many tenants in the Scottish Highlands, mostly from 1750 to 1860. The first phase involved the enclosure of the common lands – the consolidation of the smaller farms into larger farms – and the relocation of their tenants to newly created crofting communities, where they were expected to be employed in industries such as fishing, quarrying or the kelp industry. The second phase involved overcrowded crofting communities from the first phase that had lost the means to support themselves, through famine and/or collapse of industries that they had relied on, as well as continuing population growth and the expulsion of tenants, sometimes accompanied by "assisted emigration" to the industrial centers of England or abroad, where they again would have no practical choice but to submit to wage labor. This was just one of many instances that created a "reserve army of labor" necessary to create the modern working class, as a mass of individuals whose only legal means of subsistence is to sell their labor power to earn wages. Similar clearances were taking place in Ireland, too, and had occurred even earlier in England. The landlords found sheep rearing more profitable than renting land out to tenant farmers. Thomas More called it "sheep eating men."

Another implication of the idea that socialism runs counter to human nature is that humans are naturally greedy or selfish. The fact is, scientists have yet to find a gene that has greed or selfishness encoded into it, so it's not something we're naturally born with. Since it's not something we're born with, then it's strictly a behavior learned from your environment, and I doubt anyone would argue that you can't change your behavior. Is it hard? Maybe, but it's not impossible. Greed and selfishness are a byproduct of perceived scarcity; eliminate scarcity and those behaviors will disappear. It may take a while, but it'll happen. We have no other intelligent species to observe this with, so the best we can do is observe the animals that are the most genetically similar to humans – chimpanzees and bonobos, who each share about 98.7% of our DNA[78] – and see if this holds true for them. To illustrate this, you can read the following excerpt from a talk given by the late Karla Rab that gives you the answer clear as day:[79]

"Chimps and bonobos both still have habitats in the Democratic Republic of Congo, in Central Africa; but they don't share the same territory. Chimps live north of the Congo

River, and bonobos live south of it. That means chimps have to compete with other animals (notably gorillas) for scarce food resources, whereas bonobos have the southern region pretty much to themselves. That may explain why the two species evolved such different behaviors and life styles.

Chimpanzees are extremely violent. They live in groups. It is very rare for chimps to kill members of their own group, but when groups of chimps meet, the males sometimes wage all-out wars, then slaughter the infants and take the females as their own. Dominant chimpanzee mothers sometimes do away with the children of other chimps.

Chimpanzee females, like most mammals, go into heat regularly. Male chimpanzees *guard* "their" females from other males when they are in heat, fertile, to prevent them from being fertilized by a rival chimp.

Within the group, they co-operate, and they share food. Primatologist Franz de Waal has demonstrated that when food is thrown into a chimpanzee enclosure, the dominant males distribute it so that each chimp gets some, even the lowest in the hierarchy. No one goes completely hungry. De Waal has written that evolution has "etched some really basic instincts into our brains: sharing, reciprocity, and the most basic one of all: Empathy." These instincts seem to be something all primates have, including us humans.

Bonobos, unlike chimps, are very laid back. They don't use violence to settle disputes. They have what might be called a matriarchal society. Female bonobos have high status, with the dominant female and the dominant male being co-equal. The male dominance hierarchy roughly parallels the female. Females forge the alliances, and a male's rank depends on his mother's.

When groups of bonobos meet, the males hoot and stand

back while females cross over to one another in what may end up resembling an orgy. (De Waal has remarked that our [human] sexual urges are subject to such powerful moral constraints that it's hard to recognize how they permeate all aspects of our social life, and that bonobo society could teach us a lot about what human sexuality might look like without those constraints.)

No one has never seen a bonobo kill another of its own kind. Bonobo children are cared for by all the females in the group. They do have conflicts, often behaving like humans by screaming at each other and showing off their strength; but they tend to find ways actually not to harm each other, either of the same group or from a different one.

Like human women, female bonobos have "hidden ovulation" which means they don't come into heat as chimps (and most other mammals) do; no one can tell when they're fertile. Bonobos use sex not just for making babies, but as both a bonding mechanism and to reduce social tension. And because no one knows when they're fertile, male bonobos don't "guard" females when they're in heat (as chimpanzees do) so the females have more time to themselves, and more time to form female-to-female bonds.

In one experiment,* 14 bonobos (one at a time) were placed in a cage with food, flanked by two cages with no food, one of which contained a familiar group member and the other a complete stranger. The bonobos with food had the option of eating it all themselves, or to share by opening its neighbor's cage and inviting them in. Nine of the 14 individuals that took part chose to share with the stranger first. Bonobos are willing to sacrifice part of their meal "even when they themselves will not receive any benefits and might even have to pay a cost."

Both bonobos and chimps are hierarchical, but males and

females are co-equal among bonobos, where among chimps females are submissive to males. At the top of the bonobo hierarchy, there is a dominant female, not a male."

Another common argument is s that in a socialist economy no one would have any incentive to work. First off, this argument implies the common myth that capitalism incentivizes labor. The choice to either submit to wage slavery or be homeless could hardly be considered an incentive – it'd more properly be called coercion. Secondly, this ignores the fact that work was done before capitalism, and that much is done within it, for free. Socialism can't be established without a vast majority of citizens understanding that it would require all our collective cooperation. The incentive to work in a socialist economy would be the understanding that the work needs to be done to keep the system running properly. There would be no more useless, unfulfilling jobs; Every job would be a necessary part of society, and everyone would understand that and be happy to contribute.

Another argument is that socialism would suppress individual rights. First, we'd have to define exactly what should be considered a "right," because I'd argue that capitalism suppresses individual rights by allowing children to die of starvation or treatable diseases. Second, a socialist economy would be a direct democracy, where every citizen would have equal say in how the world's resources are utilized to meet everyone's needs. If we have enough resources for some people to have five houses and a yacht, then so be it, but: 1. it'd be hard to justify anyone needing that, 2. that'd be difficult to maintain without maids or robots anyway, and 3. I doubt that'd even be sustainable in the first place.

Now, if you don't consider living a right, but you consider consuming more than you need and is ecologically sustainable a right, then you're actually not concerned about individual rights at all, you're concerned about being able to satisfy your commodity fetish and fuck people over for your own benefit.

Another argument is that without price signals, resources couldn't be distributed efficiently. This implies that price signals are an efficient way to distribute resources, which is false. When almost 15,000 children under the age of 5 die of starvation every day and 1% of the world owns 47% of its wealth,[80] it's ridiculous to claim that that's efficient. Secondly, rather than having to figure out how many resources we have and converting them into prices, we'd just save ourselves the extra step by calculating everything in kind. You don't convert the ingredients in your kitchen into prices before you cook something, you just use them.

Another common argument I hear is that we don't have enough resources on the planet to sustain everyone or that the planet's overpopulated. For one, this ignores the fact that capitalism necessitates overconsumption and planned obsolescence. We would use vastly fewer resources than we do now, because production would be geared towards needs rather than wasting resources on useless products like fidget spinners and selfie sticks or products not built to last as long as possible. For two, we could use methods that aren't considered "cost effective," like vertical farming, to drastically increase our productive power. As far as overpopulation, that's a myth started by Thomas Malthus in "An Essay on the Principle of Population" in 1798. What's important to know is that 1. the world's 2010 population of about 7 billion could comfortably live on a landmass the size of Texas alone, leaving the rest of the world entirely uninhabited, and 2. the world's population will peak at about 8 billion around 2040, and then decline.[81]

To sum this all up: yes, socialism is practical. The next question is whether it's possible to establish.

How Could Socialism Be Implemented?

Assuming you believe the idea of a socialist economy to be at least somewhat practical, the next obvious question would be how it could be implemented. What could we do to get there? This is a matter of intense debate, and I understand that no one can foretell the future, so trying to give an exact blueprint would be jumping the gun, but I think we can confidently give a general idea of how it can happen.

Friedrich Engels once said in a speech that the *only* way to establish socialism is through the ballot box,[82] and I wholeheartedly agree. A violent revolution would be defeated instantly, and abstention from voting wouldn't change anything. The only way we can change the system is by informing every working-class citizen we can about the truth, the lies, the costs, and the benefits of each system, and organizing all of them to mobilize and take political action to win the upper hand for the majority so we can implement socialism. With modern technology, that's become easier to accomplish than ever before. We can inform everyone via whatever medium they prefer, be it physical books, eBooks, audiobooks, videos, seminars, you name it. After that, all it would take is all of us organizing ourselves under one political party or coalition of political parties that are truly dedicated to peacefully establishing socialism by only voting our candidates into office. Once the *vast* majority of citizens and politicians are truly socialists, the next stage will begin: the often misunderstood "dictatorship of the proletariat."

Before we go any further, it's important to understand that the word "dictatorship" had a different meaning in Karl Marx's time. Back then, it was synonymous with "political domination" or "rule," and he used the terms "dictatorship of the proletariat" and "rule of the proletariat" interchangeably. The term wasn't in contrast to democracy and wasn't synonymous with autocracy at all. Wilhelm Weitling, a colleague of Karl Marx, believed communism should be established by a single dictator,[83] and Marx actually criticized him for this.[84] What Karl Marx meant by the term was majority rule to establish socialism and abolish classes entirely, but Lenin distorted this too with his belief in political vanguardism, leading to the popular definition of the word dictator today. He believed educating the proletariat to start the revolution would take much longer than organizing a small group of specialists to start the revolution themselves and then help the proletariat get accustomed to socialism.[85] Ironically, Marx actually criticized Mikhail Bakunin for this very belief.[86] Even *more* ironically, Bakunin accused Marx of authoritarianism, even though Bakunin was secretly authoritarian and Marx, politically, was vehemently democratic.[87]

What exactly this "dictatorship" would entail would be entirely up to everyone involved at the time, but it would definitely be decided democratically and transparently to make sure it's in the interest of the vast majority. I believe that blockchain technology could potentially be the perfect platform to build a voting application that could be used to accomplish that, unless a better technology is developed by then. I don't believe that socialism can be established overnight, it would have to be a process involving lots of deliberation and action with the entire population. Karl Marx proposed some measures that may generally be applicable at the time in 'The Communist Manifesto',[88] but I'm not sure if

I agree with all of them. I believe one of the first tasks would probably be to pass laws or ratify a new constitution immediately claiming all private property as common property and installing a new administration based on bottom-up rule and full transparency. We would also need an accurate count of our population and available as well as projected resources. With that information we could then democratically decide on what to focus on producing, based on a hierarchy of our needs and capabilities,[89] and develop a plan to improve anything we may fall short on, as well as deal with any immediate threats, like pollution and greenhouse gas emissions. Once we've developed our productive capabilities enough to be able to stop using money and provide universal free access to everything, we'll have finally reached what Karl Marx referred to as the "higher" stage of communism.

How Would Socialism Be Different In Practice?

Once someone has a rough idea of how socialism could be established, their next thought would most likely be how exactly a socialist economy might be different than a capitalist economy in practice. There are too many variables to cover in-depth – and the specifics will have to be figured out by everyone involved at the time of the revolution – so I'll mainly focus on general differences and those I consider to be most important. The "first stage" would most likely be very different from the "higher stage," but they would still have at least general similarities.

First, many jobs would no longer exist. With the abolition of production for profit, various jobs would become obsolete immediately, such as insurance agents, bail bondsmen, debt collectors, stockbrokers, advertising agents, border patrol agents, financial jobs, casino jobs, cashiers, and real estate agents. Not to mention that – with the crime rate being significantly lower – our need for other jobs would decrease as a result, like security guards, military personnel, prison staff, psychologists, police officers, etc. Our need for some jobs may increase, even if only temporarily, but I doubt it would be anywhere near comparable to the number of jobs that would be done away with. With cost-cutting no longer being a factor, there also wouldn't be any intentional understaffing. Nobody would be coerced to do the work of two or more people anymore to save their slave master money. At a more advanced level, we could have at least most of the menial jobs done by robots and have a large part of our workforce focused on developing and maintaining them. Secondly, the abolition or reduced need for those jobs would also free up a vast amount of resources we could use for different purposes.

Another crucial difference is that, cost no longer being a factor, we would produce everything with the highest possible quality, efficiency, safety, and sustainability. Renewable energy that may not be "economically viable" right now could be used to increase our productivity and reduce waste. Food would be as healthy as possible. Planned obsolescence would be abolished so that electronics, vehicles, homes, furniture, etc. would be built to last as long as possible and be easily recyclable to save resources.

In addition, our workweeks would be much shorter – I've heard as little as 10 hours on average. Granted, with the system being a direct democracy, we would definitely have to dedicate a certain amount of time periodically to legislation, but, for the most part, we'd have a lot more free time to do things we enjoy, like spend time with our families or on our hobbies.

As far as everyday life is concerned, the biggest difference would be that absolutely everything would be free. No one going into crippling debt for childbirth or healthcare. No more outrageous prices on childcare, diapers, or formula. No young adults having to take out student loans to go to college or mortgages to own a home. Universal free access would eliminate all financial stress so that we could focus all our energy on improving society rather than just surviving. This would also eliminate commodity fetishism for products that are desired strictly for their perceived prestige, regardless of their actual utility. No one would want a car that only gets 15 mpg or diamonds that are acquired from child slavery. I believe this would also cause a massive shift in our social values. Instead of idolizing the rich, we would show respect to the most accomplished. The intelligent, the genuinely talented, those providing the most value to society via inventions, innovations, and scientific discoveries. Without advertising from beauty products, beauty standards would also be likely to change for the better. People would only look for valuable qualities in their partners, rather than just financial wealth.

Conclusion: Utopia?

I'm not claiming that socialism would completely solve all our problems or make the world perfect. From the beginning, we would still have behaviors like greed that may take a few generations of abundance to weed out of our society. We could still have natural disasters, rebel uprisings, psychopaths, criminals, and general errors that could cause unexpected crises. What I am claiming is that socialism can solve all the problems that are within our capacity to solve.

One of the biggest problems it would solve is war. Every war in history has been fought over ownership of resources. With all the earth's resources owned collectively and utilized democratically there would never have to be another war fought again. As a result, the military could be virtually eliminated, aside from possibly an international guard. Firearms and all other forms of war equipment would be produced on a much smaller scale, if not eventually eradicated. Not only would this free up immense amounts of resources, but it would also eliminate all the distress caused by warfare and improve humanity's overall safety and quality of life. Rather than feeling like 195 competing nations, we would all feel like one worldwide family.

Another problem that socialism would solve is that of disease. Rather than focusing our energy on developing medications that will make money, we could finally focus on finding cures to every disease possible. Rather than patients having to pay outrageous amounts of money just to stay alive, everyone will have free access to whatever medications or treatments they need. No outlandish debt for ambulance rides, insulin, sleeping pills, you name it. Not to mention much stricter regulations on addictive medications since there would be no one profiting from their sale and no doctors being offered bonuses to prescribe them.

Another major problem socialism would solve is pollution. We could finally end the rampant pollution of our air and water and destruction of our forests since it wouldn't benefit anyone any longer. We could finally focus on only using sustainable practices that won't destroy the planet in the process.

No one would have to worry about how they'll pay rent or be able to afford their next meal, let alone how we'll stop corporations from polluting the planet to save money. Perfect or not, humanity will be much better off and anyone who says otherwise is most likely focused on having power over society rather than our actual wellbeing. There isn't a single aspect of our lives that socialism wouldn't greatly improve.

It's a fact that countries with higher levels of social stratification have been linked to higher levels of obesity, mental illness, violent crime, drug addiction[90] – would you *like* me to keep going? With the abolition of classes, and, thus, social stratification, these issues would at least be far less prevalent, if not eliminated over time. Some socialists believe that the justice system would become obsolete entirely. I believe that could happen in the far future, but not immediately.

What we're talking about isn't some impossible fantasy. At one point capitalism was beneficial to society. It's allowed us to develop our productive capabilities to a level that may not have been possible under feudalism. It may have been impossible to provide for everyone's needs sufficiently before now, but just like we outgrew feudalism, we've now outgrown capitalism. We're finally capable of building a truly egalitarian society, so there's no longer any logical excuse not to. Capitalism's causing more problems than it's solving, and to not accept that and turn to our only alternative could literally cause the extinction of the entire human race.

Postscript

Once again, I'd like to thank all of you for taking the time to read this pamphlet. Many people may come across this and be too bullheaded to consider reading it at all – let alone with an open mind – so I genuinely appreciate you even giving this a chance.

Assuming I've done my job, you should understand at this point that conservatives and "democratic socialists" discussing socialism is like two critics debating a movie they've only *heard* about, and that actual socialism is practical, possible, and would be more efficient. If I'm correct, then you may naturally wonder what your next step should be. On spgb.net/3-free-standards and immediately following this section will be an offer for a free 3-month trial subscription to The Socialist Standard, the monthly journal of the Socialist Party of Great Britain, published without interruption since the party's inception in 1904. If interested, I would strongly recommend utilizing this offer so you can get further acquainted with us. Following the offer will also be our Introduction and our Declaration of Principles. I would read both for further clarification on our positions. You can also go to spgb.net and dig through some of the pages listed under the About Us and Education dropdown menus. If you'd like to join our party, you can also apply through the SPGB website. If you have any questions, the info for our various branches and contacts are also listed in this pamphlet and on spgb.net. If I haven't successfully convinced you of any of this, feel free to contact us as well. All my contact info is also on my webpage at https://bluelotusent.com/swaminetero.

Discover more about The Socialist Party of Great Britain

FREE
3-month trial
subscription
to the
socialist
standard

Or go to this link online:

https://www.worldsocialism.org/spgb/3-free-standards/

Introducing The Socialist Party

The Socialist Party advocates a society where production is freed from the artificial constraints of profit and organised for the benefit of all on the basis of material abundance. It does not have policies to ameliorate aspects of the existing social system.

The Socialist Standard is the combative monthly journal of the Socialist Party of Great Britain, published without interruption since 1904 and infuriating and exasperating political opponents in equal measure. The journal was placed on a list of publications banned for export during World War I for its call for workers not to fight for their countries, and in World War II it evaded the censor largely by producing articles on ancient wars as cover for the Party's implacable opposition to the conflict.

In the 1930s the Socialist Standard explained why capitalism would not collapse of its own accord, in response to widespread claims to the contrary, and continues to hold this view in face of the notion's recent popularity. Beveridge's welfare measures of the 1940s were viewed as a reorganisation of poverty and a necessary 'expense' of production, and Keynesian policies designed to overcome slumps an illusion. Today, the journal exposes as false the view that banks create money out of thin air, and explains why actions to prevent the depredation of the natural world can have limited effect and run counter to the nature of capitalism itself.

Gradualist reformers like the Labour Party believed that capitalism could be transformed through a series of social measures, but have merely become routine managers of the system. The Bolsheviks had to be content with developing Russian capitalism under a oneparty dictatorship. Both failures have given socialism a quite different – and unattractive – meaning: state ownership and control. As the Socialist Standard pointed out before both courses were followed, the results would more properly be called state capitalism.

The Socialist Party is not a left-wing organisation nor its journal a left-wing journal. 'Leftwing' has simply become an umbrella designation for parties and organisations demanding modifications to how we now live. The Party and the World Socialist Movement affirm that capitalism is incapable of meaningful change in the interests of the majority; that the basis of exploitation is the wages/money system. The Socialist Standard is proud to have kept alive the original idea of what socialism is – a classless, stateless, wageless, moneyless society or, defined positively, a democracy in which free and equal men and women co-operate to produce the things they need to live and enjoy life, to which they have free access in accordance with the principle 'from each according to their abilities, to each according to their needs'.

The Socialist Party, 52 Clapham High Street, London SW4 7UN

Tel: 020 7622 3811 Text: 07732 831192

spgb@worldsocialism.org spgb.net

The Companion Parties of Socialism

Socialist Party of Canada/Parti Socialiste du Canada
Box 31024, Victoria B.C. V8N 6J3 Canada.
Email: spc@worldsocialism.org

World Socialist Party (India)
257 Baghajatin 'E' Block (East), Kolkata -
700086 Tel: 033-2425-0208
Email: wspindia@hotmail.com

World Socialist Party (New Zealand)
P.O. Box 1929, Auckland, NI, New Zealand.

World Socialist Party of the United States
P.O. Box 440247, Boston, MA 02144 USA.
Email: boston@wspus.org

EUROPE

Ireland:
Cork: Kevin Cronin, 5 Curragh Woods, Frankfield, T12 KHN2, Tel: 021 4896427
Newtownabbey: Nigel McCullough, Tel: 028 90852062

Denmark: Graham Taylor, Kjaerslund 9, Floor 2 (middle), DK-8260 Viby J.

Germany: Norbert. Email: weltsozialismus@gmx.net

Italy: Gian Maria Freddi, Via Polano n. 137, 371142 Verona

Norway: Robert Stafford, Email: hallblithe@yahoo.com

Spain: Alberto Gordillo, Avenida del Parque. 2/2/3 Puerta A, 13200 Manzanares.

LATIN AMERICA

Dominican Republic: J.M. Morel, Calle 7 edif 45 apto 102, Multis Nuevo la Loteria, La Vega, Rep. Dominicana.

AFRICA

Kenya: Patrick Ndege, PO Box 13627-00100, GPO, Nairobi

Zambia: Kephas Mulenga, PO Box 280168, Kitwe.

ASIA

Japan: Michael, Email: japan.wsm@gmail.com

Australia: Trevor Clarke, Email: wspa.info@yahoo.com.au

This declaration is the basis of our organisation and, because it is also an important historical document dating from the formation of the party in 1904, its original language has been retained.

Object

The establishment of a system of society based upon the common ownership and democratic control of the means and instruments for producing and distributing wealth by and in the interest of the whole community.

Declaration of Principles

The Socialist Party of Great Britain holds:

1. That society as at present constituted is based upon the ownership of the means of living (i.e. land, factories, railways, etc.) by the capitalist or master class, and the consequent enslavement of the working class, by whose labour alone wealth is produced.

2. That in society, therefore, there is an antagonism of interests, manifesting itself as a class struggle between those who possess but do not produce and those who produce but do not possess.

3. That this antagonism can be abolished only by the emancipation of the working class from the domination of the master class, by the conversion into the common property of society of the means of production and distribution, and their democratic control by the whole people.

4. That as in the order of social evolution the working class is the last class to achieve its freedom, the emancipation of the working class will involve the emancipation of all mankind, without distinction of race or sex.

5. That this emancipation must be the work of the working class itself.

6. That as the machinery of government, including the armed forces of the nation, exists only to conserve the monopoly by the capitalist class of the wealth taken from the workers, the working class must organize consciously and politically for the conquest of the powers of government, national and local, in order that this machinery, including these forces, may be converted from an instrument of oppression into the agent of emancipation and the overthrow of privilege, aristocratic and plutocratic.

7. That as all political parties are but the expression of class interests, and as the interest of the working class is diametrically opposed to the interests of all sections of the master class, the party seeking working class emancipation must be hostile to every other party.

8. The Socialist Party of Great Britain, therefore, enters the field of political action determined to wage war against all other political parties, whether alleged labour or avowedly capitalist, and calls upon the members of the working class of this country to muster under its banner to the end that a speedy termination may be wrought to the system which deprives them of the fruits of their labour, and that poverty may give place to comfort, privilege to equality, and slavery to freedom.

References

[1] https://www.pewresearch.org/fact-tank/2018/08/07/
for-most-us-workers-real-wages-have-barely-budged-for-
decades/

[2] https://www.investopedia.com/ask/answers/101314/what-
does-current-cost-living-compare-20-years-ago.asp

[3] https://medium.com/swlh/the-rise-of-automation-and-its-
relationship-to-technical-unemployment-7ebab06b2830

[4] https://climate.nasa.gov/evidence/

[5] http://press.careerbuilder.com/2017-08-24-Living-
Paycheck-to-Paycheck-is-a-Way-of-Life-for-Majority-of-U-S-
Workers-According-to-New-CareerBuilder-Survey

[6] http://www.pewtrusts.org/~/media/assets/2015/07/reach-
of-debt-report_artfinal.pdf?la=en

[7] http://cepr.net/publications/reports/no-vacation-nation

[8] https://inequality.org/facts/wealth-inequality/

[9] https://www.nrdc.org/stories/report-million-extinctions-and-ecological-collapse-are-way

[10] https://www.lexico.com/en/definition/capitalism

[11] "Wherever there is great property there is great inequality. For one very rich man there must be at least five hundred poor, and the affluence of the few supposes the indigence of the many." -Adam Smith, The Wealth of Nations: Book V, Chapter I, Part II

https://www.marxists.org/reference/archive/smith-adam/works/wealth-of-nations/book05/ch01b.htm

[12] "In several different parts of Europe the ton or lock-duty upon a canal is the property of private persons, whose private interest obliges them to keep up the canal. If it is not kept in tolerable order, the navigation necessarily ceases altogether, and along with it the whole profit which they can make by the tolls. If those tolls were put under the management of commissioners, who had themselves no interest in them, they might be less attentive to the maintenance of the works which produced them." -Adam Smith, The Wealth of Nations: Book V, Chapter I, Part III, Article I

https://www.marxists.org/reference/archive/smith-adam/works/wealth-of-nations/book05/ch01c.htm

[13] "It is in this manner that money has become in all civilised nations the universal instrument of commerce, by the intervention of which goods of all kinds are bought and sold, or exchanged for one another." -Adam Smith, The Wealth of Nations: Book I, Chapter IV

https://www.marxists.org/reference/archive/smith-adam/works/wealth-of-nations/book01/ch04.htm

[14] "A man must always live by his work, and his wages must at least be sufficient to maintain him. They must even upon most occasions be somewhat more; otherwise it would be impossible for him to bring up a family, and the race of such workmen could not last beyond the first generation." -Adam Smith, The Wealth of Nations: Book I, Chapter VIII

https://www.marxists.org/reference/archive/smith-adam/works/wealth-of-nations/book01/ch08.htm

[15] "But when barter ceases, and money has become the common instrument of commerce, every particular commodity is more frequently exchanged for money than for any other commodity." -Adam Smith, The Wealth of Nations: Book I, Chapter V

https://www.marxists.org/reference/archive/smith-adam/works/wealth-of-nations/book01/ch05.htm

[16] "It seldom happens that the person who tills the ground has wherewithal to maintain himself till he reaps the harvest. His maintenance is generally advanced to him from the stock of a master, the farmer who employs him, and who would have no interest to employ him, unless he was to share in the produce of his labour, or unless his stock was to be replaced to him with a profit." -Adam Smith, The Wealth of Nations: Book I, Chapter VIII

https://www.marxists.org/reference/archive/smith-adam/works/wealth-of-nations/book01/ch08.htm

[17] "The affluence of the rich excites the indignation of the poor, who are often both driven by want, and prompted by envy, to invade his possessions. It is only under the shelter of the civil magistrate that the owner of that valuable property, which is acquired by the labour of many years, or perhaps of many successive generations, can sleep a single night in

security. He is at all times surrounded by unknown enemies, whom, though he never provoked, he can never appease, and from whose injustice he can be protected only by the powerful arm of the civil magistrate continually held up to chastise it. The acquisition of valuable and extensive property, therefore, necessarily requires the establishment of civil government. Where there is no property, or at least none that exceeds the value of two or three days' labour, civil government is not so necessary." -Adam Smith, The Wealth of Nations: Book V, Chapter I, Part II

https://www.marxists.org/reference/archive/smith-adam/works/wealth-of-nations/book05/ch01b.htm

[18] "The causes or circumstances which naturally introduce subordination, or which naturally, and antecedent to any civil institution, give some men some superiority over the greater part of their brethren, seem to be four in number.

The first of those causes or circumstances is the superiority of personal qualifications, of strength, beauty, and agility of body; of wisdom and virtue, of prudence, justice, fortitude, and moderation of mind. (…)

The second of those causes or circumstances is the superiority of age. (…)

The third of those causes or circumstances is the superiority of fortune. (…)

The fourth of those causes or circumstances is the superiority of birth.

https://www.marxists.org/reference/archive/smith-adam/works/wealth-of-nations/book05/ch01b.htm

[19] "What are the common wages of labour, depends

everywhere upon the contract usually made between those two parties, whose interests are by no means the same. The workmen desire to get as much, the masters to give as little as possible. The former are disposed to combine in order to raise, the latter in order to lower the wages of labour."
-Adam Smith, The Wealth of Nations: Book I, Chapter VIII

https://www.marxists.org/reference/archive/smith-adam/works/wealth-of-nations/book01/ch08.htm

[20] https://www.epi.org/publication/epidemic-wage-theft-costing-workers-hundreds/

[21] https://www.cbsnews.com/news/the-madoff-scam-meet-the-liquidator-25-09-2009/

[22] https://www.worldsocialism.org/spgb/socialist-standard/2010s/2019/no-1377-may-2019/boeing-the-fatal-price-of-competition/

[23] https://www.worldhunger.org/world-child-hunger-facts/

[24] https://www.worldvision.org/hunger-news-stories/food-waste

[25] https://www.air.org/resource/americas-youngest-outcasts-report-card-child-homelessness

[26] https://www.lincolninst.edu/publications/policy-focus-reports/empty-house-next-door

[27] https://www.cbsnews.com/news/2018-taxes-some-of-americas-biggest-companies-paid-little-to-no-federal-income-tax-last-year/

[28] https://www.cbsnews.com/news/how-low-wage-employers-cost-taxpayers-153-billion-a-year/

[29] https://www.lexico.com/en/definition/socialism

[30] "Thus, to a certain extent, the history of the [Communist] Manifesto reflects the history of the modern working-class movement since 1848. At present, it is doubtless the most widely circulated, the most international product of all socialist literature, the common programme of many millions of workers of all countries from Siberia to California." -Friedrich Engels, Preface to the 1890 German Edition

https://www.marxists.org/archive/marx/works/1848/communist-manifesto/preface.htm#preface-1890

[31] "Right, by its very nature, can consist only in the application of an equal standard; but unequal individuals (and they would not be different individuals if they were not unequal) are measurable only by an equal standard insofar as they are brought under an equal point of view, are taken from one definite side only -- for instance, in the present case, are regarded only as workers and nothing more is seen in them, everything else being ignored. Further, one worker is married, another is not; one has more children than another, and so on and so forth. Thus, with an equal performance of labor, and hence an equal in the social consumption fund, one will in fact receive more than another, one will be richer than another, and so on. To avoid all these defects, right, instead of being equal, would have to be unequal.

But these defects are inevitable in the first phase of communist society as it is when it has just emerged after prolonged birth pangs from capitalist society. Right can never be higher than the economic structure of society and its cultural development conditioned thereby.

In a higher phase of communist society, after the enslaving subordination of the individual to the division of labor, and therewith also the antithesis between mental and physical labor, has vanished;

after labor has become not only a means of life but life's prime want; after the productive forces have also increased with the all-around development of the individual, and all the springs of co-operative wealth flow more abundantly -- only then then can the narrow horizon of bourgeois right be crossed in its entirety and society inscribe on its banners: From each according to his ability, to each according to his needs!" -Karl Marx, Critique of the Gotha Programme, Part I

https://www.marxists.org/archive/marx/works/1875/gotha/ch01.htm

[32] "But the scientific distinction between socialism and communism is clear. What is usually called socialism was termed by Marx the "first", or lower, phase of communist society." -Vladimir Lenin, The State and Revolution, Chapter V, Part IV

https://www.marxists.org/archive/lenin/works/1917/staterev/ch05.htm#s4

[33] "The distinguishing feature of Communism is not the abolition of property generally, but the abolition of bourgeois property. But modern bourgeois private property is the final and most complete expression of the system of producing and appropriating products, that is based on class antagonisms, on the exploitation of the many by the few.

In this sense, the theory of the Communists may be summed up in the single sentence: Abolition of private property.

We Communists have been reproached with the desire of abolishing the right of personally acquiring property as the fruit of a man's own labour, which property is alleged to be the groundwork of all personal freedom, activity and independence.

Hard-won, self-acquired, self-earned property! Do you mean the property of petty artisan and of the small peasant, a form of property that preceded the bourgeois form? There is no need to abolish that; the development of industry has to a great extent already destroyed it, and is still destroying it daily.

Or do you mean the modern bourgeois private property?

But does wage-labour create any property for the labourer? Not a bit. It creates capital, i.e., that kind of property which exploits wage-labour, and which cannot increase except upon condition of begetting a new supply of wage-labour for fresh exploitation.

(...)

When, therefore, capital is converted into common property, into the property of all members of society, personal property is not thereby transformed into social property. It is only the social character of the property that is changed. It loses its class character." -Karl Marx, Manifesto of The Communist Party: Chapter II

https://www.marxists.org/archive/marx/works/1848/communist-manifesto/ch02.htm

[34] "Finally, when all capital, all production, all exchange have been brought together in the hands of the nation, private property will disappear of its own accord, money will become superfluous, and production will so expand and man so change that society will be able to slough off whatever of its old economic habits may remain." -Friedrich Engels, The Principles of Communism: Question 18

https://www.marxists.org/archive/marx/works/1847/11/prin-com.htm

[35] "Trades Unions work well as centers of resistance against the encroachments of capital. They fail partially from an injudicious use of their power. They fail generally from limiting themselves to a guerilla war against the effects of the existing system, instead of simultaneously trying to change it, instead of using their organized forces as a lever for the final emancipation of the working class that is to say the ultimate abolition of the wages system." -Karl Marx, 'Value, Price, and Profit., Chapter XIV

https://www.marxists.org/archive/marx/works/1865/value-price-profit/ch03.htm#c14

[36] "With the seizing of the means of production by society, production of commodities is done away with, and, simultaneously, the mastery of the product over the producer." -Friedrich Engels, Socialism: Utopian and Scientific, Part III

https://www.marxists.org/archive/marx/works/1880/soc-utop/ch03.htm

[37] "When, in the course of development, class distinctions have disappeared, and all production has been concentrated in the hands of a vast association of the whole nation, the public power will lose its political character. Political power, properly so called, is merely the organised power of one class for oppressing another. If the proletariat during its contest with the bourgeoisie is compelled, by the force of circumstances, to organise itself as a class, if, by means of a revolution, it makes itself the ruling class, and, as such, sweeps away by force the old conditions of production, then it will, along with these conditions, have swept away the conditions for the existence of class antagonisms and of classes generally, and will thereby have abolished its own supremacy as a class.

In place of the old bourgeois society, with its classes and

class antagonisms, we shall have an association, in which the free development of each is the condition for the free development of all." -Karl Marx, Manifesto of The Communist Party: Chapter II

https://www.marxists.org/archive/marx/works/1848/communist-manifesto/ch02.htm

[38] "As soon as there is no longer any social class to be held in subjection; as soon as class rule, and the individual struggle for existence based upon our present anarchy in production, with the collisions and excesses arising from these, are removed, nothing more remains to be repressed, and a special repressive force, a State, is no longer necessary." -Friedrich Engels, Socialism: Utopian and Scientific, Part III

https://www.marxists.org/archive/marx/works/1880/soc-utop/ch03.htm

[39] "It presupposes, therefore, the development of production carried out to a degree at which appropriation of the means of production and of the products, and, with this, of political domination, of the monopoly of culture, and of intellectual leadership by a particular class of society, has become not only superfluous but economically, politically, intellectually, a hindrance to development." -Friedrich Engels, Socialism: Utopian and Scientific, Part III

https://www.marxists.org/archive/marx/works/1880/soc-utop/ch03.htm

[40] https://www.lexico.com/en/definition/effective_demand

[41] https://berniesanders.com/issues/demand-that-the-wealthy-large-corporations-and-wall-street-pay-their-fair-share-in-taxes/

[42] https://berniesanders.com/issues/real-wall-street-reform/

[43] https://berniesanders.com/issues/fair-banking-for-all/

[44] https://berniesanders.com/issues/fight-for-working-families/

[45] https://berniesanders.com/issues/health-care-for-all/

[46] https://berniesanders.com/issues/college-for-all/

[47] https://berniesanders.com/issues/get-big-money-out-of-politics-and-restore-democracy/

[48] https://www.worldsocialism.org/spgb/our-object-and-declaration-principles/

[49] https://fee.org/articles/the-myth-of-scandinavian-socialism/

[50] "...the socialist labor party of Germany endeavors by every lawful means to bring about a free state and a socialistic society, to effect the destruction of the iron law of wages by doing away with the system of wage labor, to abolish exploitation of every kind, and to extinguish all social and political inequality."

https://history.hanover.edu/texts/gotha.html

[51] http://ghdi.ghi-dc.org/sub_document.cfm?document_id=3049

[52] https://www.britannica.com/topic/Speenhamland-system

[53] https://ocasio-cortez.house.gov/gnd

[54] https://climate.nasa.gov/evidence/

[55] https://climate.nasa.gov/causes/

[56] https://www.theguardian.com/environment/2018/oct/08/global-warming-must-not-exceed-15c-warns-landmark-un-report

[57] https://climate.nasa.gov/effects/

[58] https://ourworldindata.org/how-much-will-it-cost-to-mitigate-climate-change

[59] https://www.cbc.ca/news/politics/liberals-carbon-price-lower-1.4769530

[60] https://www.vice.com/en_us/article/7xgymg/planting-billions-of-trees-isnt-going-to-stop-climate-change

[61] https://www.dailymail.co.uk/sciencetech/article-7350713/Bill-Gates-wants-spray-millions-tonnes-dust-stratosphere-stop-global-warming.html?ito=social-facebook&fbclid=IwAR0XT6VQ_GgNDkFUyLY0mRH65MYFPObbMFrrhsc1mwHw6SxYfcx10omtYYU&fbclid=IwAR1_ObcsMgFXUqALEEpQ9eSaSdpUF5TuHr2CMShbIByfdzMssKyZsuLVBNc

[62] https://bipartisanpolicy.org/blog/direct-air-capture-key-takeaways-from-the-national-academies-report-on-negative-emission-technologies/

[63] http://www.geoengineeringmonitor.org/2018/05/direct-air-capture/

[64] https://www.worldsocialism.org/spgb/socialist-standard/1910s/1918/no-168-august-1918/the-revolution-in-russia-where-it-fails/
[65] "It has not occurred to them that state capitalism would

be a step forward as compared with the present state of affairs in our Soviet Republic. If in approximately six months' time state capitalism became established in our Republic, this would be a great success and a sure guarantee that within a year socialism will have gained a permanently firm hold and will have become invincible in our country.

...

No one, I think, in studying the question of the economic system of Russia, has denied its transitional character. Nor, I think, has any Communist denied that the term Socialist Soviet Republic implies the determination of Soviet power to achieve the transition to socialism, and not that the new economic system is recognised as a socialist order." -Vladimir Lennin, "Left-Wing" Childishness, Part III

https://www.marxists.org/archive/lenin/works/1918/may/09.htm

[66] https://www.globalsecurity.org/military/world/russia/industry-stalin-1fyp.htm

[67] https://www.encyclopedia.com/history/encyclopedias-almanacs-transcripts-and-maps/cooperatives-law

[68] http://countrystudies.us/china/87.htm

[69] http://countrystudies.us/china/92.htm

[70] http://revolutions.truman.edu/cuba/interest.htm

[71] https://www.ascecuba.org/asce_proceedings/comparison-of-international-monetary-fund-and-world-bank-conditionalities-and-cubas-economic-reforms-of-the-1990s/

[72] http://world.kbs.co.kr/special/northkorea/contents/archives/outline/outline_1950.htm?lang=e

[73] https://ir.lawnet.fordham.edu/ilj/vol27/iss4/2/

[74] https://www.aporrea.org/actualidad/a165136.html

[75] https://www.bea.gov/system/files/2019-07/gdpind119.pdf - Page 13

[76] "... the communist revolution will not merely be a national phenomenon but must take place simultaneously in all civilized countries..." -Friedrich Engels, The Principles of Communism: Question 19

https://www.marxists.org/archive/marx/works/1847/11/princom.htm

[77] https://openjournals.library.sydney.edu.au/index.php/JSSSH/article/view/9084

[78] https://www.guinnessworldrecords.com/world-records/most-genetically-similar-animal-to-humans/

[79] http://www.wspus.org/2017/01/human-nature-and-how-it-can-save-us/

[80] https://www.cnbc.com/2018/11/19/how-much-money-it-takes-to-be-among-the-richest-50-percent-worldwide.html

[81] https://overpopulationisamyth.com/episode-1-overpopulation-the-making-of-a-myth/

[82] "We want the abolition of classes. What is the means of achieving it? The only means is political domination of the proletariat.

...

The political freedoms, the right of assembly and association, and the freedom of the press — those are our weapons." - Friedrich Engels, Apropos Of Working-Class Political Action

https://www.marxists.org/archive/marx/works/1871/09/21.htm

[83] https://books.google.com/books?id=A0hRBAAAQBAJ&pg=PT150&lpg=PT150&dq=if+we+bring+about+communism+through+revolutionary+means+then+we+must+have+a+dictator+who+holds+sway+over+all+weitling&source=bl&ots=vp1_a6Onmj&sig=ACfU3U1aOoQFeuOCyZU7yNLPi LNiXYgfrA&hl=en&sa=X&ved=2ahUKEwiOv7bS69TjAhV PuZ4KHZeNDH4Q6AEwAHoECAkQAQ#v=onepage&q= if%20we%20bring%20about%20communism%20through%20 revolutionary%20means%20then%20we%20must%20 have%20a%20dictator%20who%20holds%20sway%20 over%20all%20weitling&f=false

[84] https://books.google.com/books?id=A0hRBAAAQBAJ &pg=PT60&dq=the+desire+to+carry+through+a+system+i nvolving+a+single+head+in+the+dictatorship+deserves+to +be+called+nonsense&hl=en&sa=X&ved=0ahUKEwi6rbqr-tTjAhXL6Z4KHWfDB5UQ6AEIKjAA#v=onepage&q=the%20 desire%20to%20carry%20through%20a%20system%20 involving%20a%20single%20head%20in%20the%20 dictatorship%20deserves%20to%20be%20called%20 nonsense&f=false

[85] "If Socialism can only be realised when the intellectual development of all the people permits it, then we shall not see Socialism for at least five hundred years…. The Socialist political party—this is the vanguard of the working-class; it must not allow itself to be halted by the lack of education of the mass average, but it must lead the masses, using the Soviets as organs of revolutionary initiative…. But in order to lead the wavering, the comrades Left Socialist Revolutionaries themselves must stop hesitating…." -Vladimir Lenin

https://www.marxists.org/archive/reed/1919/10days/10days/ch12.htm

[86] "To assure the success of the revolution one must have "unity of thought and action". The members of the International are trying to create this unity by propaganda, by discussion and the public organisation of the proletariat. But all Bakunin needs is a secret organisation of one hundred people, the privileged representatives of the revolutionary idea, the general staff in the background, self-appointed and commanded by the permanent "Citizen B". Unity of thought and action means nothing but orthodoxy and blind obedience. Perinde ac cadaver.* We are indeed confronted with a veritable Society of Jesus.

To say that the hundred international brothers must "serve as intermediaries between the revolutionary idea and the popular instincts," is to create and unbridgeable gulf between the Alliance's revolutionary idea and the proletarian masses; it means proclaiming that these hundred guardsmen cannot be recruited anywhere but from among the privileged classes." -Page 112 of attached PDF

https://libcom.org/library/anarchism-anarcho-syndicalism-selected-writings-marx-engels-lenin

[87] https://libcom.org/library/marx-bakunin-question-authoritarianism

[88] https://www.marxists.org/archive/marx/works/1848/communist-manifesto/ch02.htm

[89] https://www.worldsocialism.org/spgb/socialist-standard/2010s/2019/no-1380-august-2019/socialism-and-planning-part2-feedback/

[90] https://www.jrf.org.uk/report/does-income-inequality-cause-health-and-social-problems

Bio

I don't know if this counts as an accolade, but one time I had to walk 6 miles after I missed the bus. 10/10 do not recommend. I grew up homeless on and off and on welfare most of my childhood, so poverty's the homie. Some people call him the "downside" of capitalism, but I call him "building character." I was also raised in Las Vegas, Nevada, so I'm definitely judging your tacos. I have the cutest daughter to ever live, this isn't up for debate. When I'm not making music, I'm either cussing profusely on Call of Duty, binging on an RPG, or arguing on Twitter. Follow me I guess?

https://bluelotusent.com/swaminetero

www.ingramcontent.com/pod-product-compliance
Lightning Source LLC
Chambersburg PA
CBHW051038030426
42336CB00015B/2935